TIDE

POETRY

TIDE

POETRY

BY

JOHNSON NGUYEN

ISBN 978-0-9985737-2-4 (Paperback Edition)

Library of Congress Control Number 2017900098

Book Design by Anh L. Pham
Front Cover Art by Paul Wilford
Photography by Minh-Quan Nguyen

Printed and bound in the United States of America
First Edition

1 2 3 4 20 19 18 17

Available from Amazon.com and other retail outlets

Cheese Lobster Publishing | Dallas, TX

CHEESE LOBSTER
PUBLISHING

For my wife, Lan Anh
who inspires and
nurtures my body
creative mind
meaningful soul
into a positive force
with delightful perspective
and purpose
each and every day

PREFACE

Creative writing provides solace, direction, inspiration and confirmation in my times of need. It is an integral part of my being and a continuous, valuable process. After all, there is a poem and story hiding at every corner! At times the urge to capture a thought is so great it forces me to pull over on the side of the road. They must be captured quickly and immortalized or else might vanish for good.

Tide symbolizes my own creativity, attitude, ideologies, philosophies, experimentation, hedonism, individualism, autonomy, culture and characterization. It reminds me to live a productive, positive and meaningful life for which nothing is more important. When the sea is rough I sit alone on the edge of the dock and tune into this ebb and flow channel and realize that life will ever be violent high and docile low tides. It is how we deal with this volatility that defines our existence.

The power and magic of poetry is that you bend them to fit your own experience and understanding. Much the same as fine impressionist art they invoke and demand emotion. Each of these works have personal purpose and meaning to me. They are shared in hopes that you will find and feel a common connection, in your own individualistic way. Come closer. Open up your mind. Sit beside me. Know your place in this vast world. Know who will be by your side. We all have much to be blessed with and much to offer our society and humanity. Through the capricious years my most important discovery to date—never again will I *have* to sit alone.

CONTENTS

I

II

III

IV

VII

I

BLOOM

Humble differences set aside
On my mind a visual realized
All that is beautiful
Shrouded of natural wonderment
Cautioned by eager winds
Which carve hard faces
And the time passed watching choice
As if flowers were in bloom

SWING

Stay as kind as you ever were
As you will ever be in future memories
And as the swift seasons pass
Disguised as blessings
From time to thoughtful time
Once in a blue while we are reminded
How the fabric of friends
And the seams of close knit family
Become the steady oak tree
You swing from

IMPRESSION

We stand proud before picture peerless
friendship in a gold gallery frame. Our
spirited lives hanging in the utmost secure
and prestigious museum of natural thought.
Still, our authentic prize lies in the pervasive
understanding and care we have shown
each other over the meaningful years—this,
the longest lasting impression.

UNSAID

In all the speech we share and direct
That dare to affect paper skin bonds
From thin air to ambivalent sound
That shows intention on invisible meters
That may have viable truths untested
Resting on shoulders of white lab coats
That muffle under water pressure
That fill up colorful balloons
That which encompasses
All final analysis of human behavior
Solely displayed by the
Compiled actions
Of our words unsaid

TREE IN SILHOUETTE

Often alone, but not lonely
Friends surround this old tree
Wind whispers neighborhood gossip aloud
I waver with Laughter incessantly

Fickle Rain visits by chance
Grass, Soil, intertwine in dance
If ever two Loved—thee
Gazing below, green with Envy

Ominous Sun of warmth, glee
Birds perch and preach melodies
In your complete absence I
Would Die! My dearest companion

Then Night turns chameleon Skies
Lie under Moon's watchful eye
Life friends—all I need
Alone, but not lonely indeed

PERILLA

Turn back agile hands
Many faces to remember
Those stills to reminisce
These perceived content memories

Inhale deeply from within
Success realizes good deeds
My meaning character lively
Unforgettable fresh red perilla

A WRITER'S PRAYER

Before the bones in my hands become too brittle.
Before my legs are too weak to support a young
man.
Before my joints disintegrate and become
clustered, confused.
Before pain bullies my emotions into
handing over my intellect and sanity.
Give me the strength in body and resolve
in soul to see it through.
Bestow upon me the power to
transcend mediocrity and achieve
greatness my own world unknown.
Provide me shelter, protection, and
good fortune for this task of mine,
and of yours.

That is all I ask of you.

GRACE

$\mathcal{Q}$uietly sitting at a round table our family says grace before the first bite of food is taken. We join hands with the person to the left and to the right. Respect the tradition, the cause, the outcome and the family name. You pledge not for yourself but reasons much greater than your own self agenda, gain or worth.

This Nation is our mankind family as well. The globe, our extended family. We all have children's futures in our lives, we all have lives ending each day, we all have responsibilities as human kind. Disease, death, disaster do not discriminate; hate, ignorance and apathy are willful decisions of pitiful men who do not respect any process, freedom nor order.

Only on the backs of angelic individuals, selfless organizations and compassionate governments will change commence. Imagine how buildings will be erected higher and stronger than before. We fight not amongst each other but band as one for an unforgettable performance of peace—faith of the people will be restored. Whether for natural, unnatural, or supernatural causes, it is mankind who

will have to sift through the rubble, lift the heavy stones, sweep the dust of fallen buildings and brittle bones. One country, one race, one group, one man cannot achieve this alone.

To survive treachery of this magnitude we must work in tandem and pull our resources together. Our diverse brigade shall have people from all different colors, walks and sizes passing buckets of strength, motivation, and promise from one to another, collectively extinguishing this raging fire of disparity and chaos.

If we cannot send needed supplies, then we shall send clothes. If not clothes then food. If not food then medicine. And if not medicine then we shall send our thoughts! They are going to need beyond our capability. Saying grace and having grace are two greatly different notions. Part of the human condition is understanding when and where our help is most needed. Every person deserves to eat quietly with their own family.

[Dedicated to the 2010 Haiti Earthquake victims and their families]

INSPIRE

A firm affirmation for all
That we are in command
Of our own demand
At any time
Is there not a new opportunity
At every dawn
Or waking moment?
To make it right
If ill feelings
Have not quite left
Promise
Stand still only briefly
Travel light in mind—
We all have baggage
Know they can be rolled
Alongside these fine days
Remember to embrace
And be secure in them
A long way to have come
Keep what we find
In deserve
If ever in doubt of shadow
Hug a mirror
Clearly see
Who you should
And ever on inspire

CAULK

Waiting all day for a red light
The sound of your voice
Through the receiver
Speaks my name
And I will jump
And I will run
Sit down next to me
Take it out on me
Tears are exciting to see
Especially when they roll
Like paper
We shall wait patiently
On the whether
Your hand handled
By mine
Through the
Crowded nights
Of all the variables
To keep
Our brand of love apart
Distance, timing, assets and flesh
That which cannot be fixed
A beaded line
Steadily laid against
The sink holes of uncertainty
In caulk

CANDLE

Far removed from the slant on tradition
To be safer than the next or rather plain afraid
Competing in the field for the same prize
That lies within
Champion companion
Ship to set sail with
But to fight
Stay and fight
Not so nice
Imagine at day break
How they must brighten up your face
Holding a candle

ERRAND

Thoughts of you derived.
What time is it—I miss you.
Miss how you talked like the sun and walked on the
bright side. Miss our innocent fun and miles of bike
ride. Have we ever the ones to tire of each other,
engage in petty arguments or not speak with young
minds and hearts on our sleeves, but rather harness
pure sincere admiration for one another.
We take for granted our travels in this lifetime.
We take for granted how we travel.
We take for granted with whom we travel.
Can't feel the breath of faith into these
exhausted lungs any longer, can't feel the stare of
self-consciousness out the corner of my own eye
any longer.
At last to finally go home,
at last to join my best friend,
at last my final errand.

[Dedicated to Aaron Wilford and his family]

II

TREASURE

Natural and pleasant our reaction
Finding that which is dear to us—
    Lyrics in a song
    Lines from the cinema
    Metal on the ground
    Shells from the beach
    Canvas on a wall
    Paper in the wind
        Value is what one places in it
        Its worth is how long one holds onto it
        The greatest meaning gifts
        Arrive when not searching for it
            Career
            Friends
            Opportunities
            And the one
                Treasure

FIRE

A year of violent beta in our markets,
homes and eventful lives but the longer
I live the more apparent to me how the
spirit of the holidays are best captured
by the familiar characters around the fire.

FROZEN TREES

The weather withers
Your long fellow stems—
A function of feelings

Perceived by the sun
And of the moon
But soon you realize
Seasons change at will
Usually too short or long

Yet you bark back on deaf ears
In the end our skin
Sheds just enough
To keep the disappointment from
Adhering to our souls

So we stand rooted
Waving arms up high
Toward other frozen trees

F CHORD

Years of strumming
With these callus fingertips
Have yet to learn
Their lesson

Against the metal grain
Dirty vibrations resonate
Warm ear pressed up against
Well crafted hardwood

And as the precious age
Harsh tones soften
To sound more refined
More distinguished and wise

Persistency of progress
In the name of production—
Notably striking
Abstruse F Chord

ENDEAVOR

The virtue of patience
And meaningful Love—
The most admirably deserved
Among us all
The joyous journey
Between two hearts
And minds
Who become
One endeavor

TEARS

Inland devastation of innovation
Order and poised excellence
View ship wrecked shores
Once proud structures tumbled
Floating despair of the detached
Agony amongst the
Slowly walking

This ambitious tide
Cleansed hope
Cleansed confidence
Shifted the Earth
And human
Beliefs

But I alone spot an amaryllis flower
At the epicenter
Standing tall amidst
The grey rubble and darkness
Unwashed away
By the tsunami
Of tears

[Dedicated to the 2011 Japan Tsunami victims and their families]

FLOOD GATES

Filling up fast
In front of our sad, eager eyes
Every solitary salty tear shed
Absorbed into hedonistic Heaven above
Rightfully returns
To the emotional Earth
As rain drops
Which form the aftermath
Of open flood gates

DETRIMENT

Accomplishments often offset
Through the darkening of skies
And times
A light eventually emerges
Eyes need time to adjust
To the white balance
Just as you once did
The swing attacks
Both sides
Each pass less
In force
Than the last
Know this
Make it easier
Handle the down turns
The difference in attitude
Positively weighs heavily
On the well being
Of one's detriment

HONEY

Ingest saliva
As the injustice unfolds
Fogs handheld mirrors
Story begins with lies
Began with a device
Retribution with absolution
Married to the ties that bind
In no kind words
Left with the burden
Handle the bill
Carry the cross
Across the sea
See what you have done
Lest we forget the past
But how we remember
Torture the man
Torch the village
Burn it down
Build the ground up
Again
Tomorrow
We die
We love
We lived
Swear
To tell
Our story
Intact
Honest honey

SAVIOR

Violent winds
Blow the mosquito
Which carry the virus
That changes
The game
The one
That changes
Man kind
And its world
Population
Growth bacteria
Enamored
Halted
Salt of the Earth
Unbound from the sea
Of bodies
Of mind
Of sound
Relentless
As the tides
Which pulls slowly
From the moon
Dark galaxy above
Magma below
Rock in between
Water kept inside

Black oil
Pockets found
Hope lost
Host found
To be this honest
To be this close
The coffin
Adorned with engravings
Marked with paint
Cherished for ever on
Buried above
Buried alive
Resist the urge
To die alone
But for a cause
Save for fairness
Save for death
Save for you
Savior in us

FREE

Bring the chagrin to haptic gatherings
No one entertains sorrow quite like you
And standing around do you realize
We are so much alike—bitter and defiant
There is still no running up glass walls
Trapped until it breaks
Until it gives into our favor
Until boredom causes a stir
Until good graces at last
Set us free

ACCLAIM

Blue Jay infiltrates my serious mind
Dancing about the sky
Under lattice shade
Reaching tree branches
Perches on the edge
Reminds me
Can't see the forest
For the trees indeed

Start looking up, like Things
Otherwise miss birds' flight in concord
Miss Sun play
Miss childhood games
Miss out

How change in thought
Opens up dimensions in reality
Through the consistent glass
Of reflection and perception
Find meaning in puzzles and series
Decipher how pixel colors
Can seem a little brighter
To create an amazing story
Your future much the same
On the other side of acclaim

STREET

May be daunting
Might be frightening
The first step outside
Your comfort zone
Down the hall
Heavy door
Lock
In the way
Points to the road
Where concrete shoes belong
This way
A start
This is somewhere
It is now
Did you ask the time?
To know or no?
Choose the former
Choose wisely
And without regret—
You will get there
Go
It took the surreal
Boldini two bold years
To cross the street

COFFEE CUPS

Where I may be a fool in person
Future envisioned
The world knows
Not of it being ruled tonight
Slayed by two all too naturally
Elegance and delight sustained
Speech conveyed in warm tones
Smiles sparkling
Laughter intriguing
Bodies leaning
Audible hearts resting
On the paper sleeves
Of coffee cups

III

RECLUSE

How close are we
The end of time
Not of rainbows beyond
The horizon through
The looking glass
Save for barriers
And prisons
That hide from inelastic
Demand bones
In recluse

GUN

Riot on paper
Riot on blank screens where they exist
Stay alive long enough
To dull the saw
That keeps cutting down
Forward progress
For the children
On our watch—
It is our responsibility
That which keeps
Beating
Singing
Fighting
Reveals our deepest
Reason
You can't kill
That with a gun

WHEEL

Mind less feeling
One less to worry about
From the long laundry list
Of anxiety
Betrayal in the slightest
Harm full
Event full
On account of self-realization
The urge to forget
The object
Of infatuation
When yielding
To spinning the wheel

LUXURY

Haunted by working title and as of late
Plotting pure career suicidal tendencies
Reconsider angles and tactics
Attack the mundane but be weary
Heresy and hearsay
To be here
Important discovery—
Ahead of the masses
Among the many
Who plead and beg
Wait and wait
No waiter to check up on
Seams that do not hold up
Where salt water soaks through
Where struggles lie
What becomes of tragic thoughts
Save for action or mobility
Time for food
Time for drink
Time for bed
Time for healing
Time spent in
Unusual luxury

LENDER

Borrowed soul and borrowed salvation
Ring true the tone of self-sacrificing shame
Immersed in the plight of humility
And humiliation we do learn—or do we?
Time not spent, rather derived
Out of pity by higher men
Meaningless change
Peace of mind and original intellect
Now old paint laden by capitalistic hogs
Which is branded primer in semi-gloss
From ashes and bare feet
A filthy slave to find profound value in self—
The keen eye for misstep
An ear for harsh baby cries
A muscular back to withstand
Landmark lashings of an unforgivable society
Although their tools reach long
Evolve and whip with the sound of firecracker pop
Their witty degradations
And slurs extremely sharp
Eyes glare with increasing dehumanizing contempt
Using the salty song of our bloody limbs
We must carry on the financial plantation
Of the wealthy lender

UNDERWRITER

You think exactly about
What you wish not to think about
Get used to the sound of broken for the time being—
Fans, belts, hearts and spirits
Severed links, whether human touch or internet
Common as ladybugs
Happen without warrant
Notice or justification
Purchase anything these days
Buy some time
And spend wisely
While in your sheltering cave
Hold on stalactite
This too shall pass
But it could take a relatively long while
Life is about the small difference
What you want to be
Where you want to be
How you want to be
The odd journey it takes to get you
To those many rewarding points
We fit into slim brackets
Adjust figures as follows

Often represented by ratios and percentiles
We are never stationery numbers
It is not the sum
Of credit ratings
Private placements
Nor current disposition
That judges character
Know how quickly the tides can change—
Wealth, attitude, bonds and luck
Know that good people deeds
Always worth purchasing
Understand these fundamentals guidelines
Rhetorical underwriter

BLAST

The explosion was unfair—
We weren't ready
Hair and skin
All burnt
The flood of humans
With tears to mix
Line of pain
Line of sight
Beholden to deaf ears
So I found them
And sat the guilty up
Set their matter on fire
Atop the concrete
Following the blast

[Dedicated to the 2013 Boston Marathon victims and their families]

GONE

In my mind
Violent crime ensues
Apparent suicide
Decidedly bottles
Pressed powder
Brand Martini
Here and there
Saltwater on steel
Beautiful still scene
Heavy lids
To oblivion
What did die
That knight
Not a man
But angry soul
Move forward
Let go of hate
Let go of pettiness
Obtainable goal
Climb out of the hole
Time to make amends
Make up life
For years have come
And gone

HOOK

Search lights
Horizon night sky
Ponder
To strive for that original idea
Sit idly in thought
The kind
That lives
Within a person
Soul
The kind
That gives off hue
For a life time
The kind
That glows immortality
Wonder
And demands of you
Discover hook

MEMBER

Through rose
Lenses
Eyes focus in

Research is undoubted
Search again
Insane

Hat trick
Lies about lying
Ghastly

Justice
Universe to obtain
Self-Righteous

Enjoy mass
Consequences of this
Member

PETS

Through our
Comfort window
Out onto the cautious
Limbs
Bird's eye
Glaring at the bleak
These grotesque
Dead
Walking
Pets

BLANKETS

Tension in the muscles
Sensitive to surroundings
Out of patience
Sense pressure coming from the corner of my eye
Time to abide by the laws that govern action
Against societal discord
Which breeds discontent
And calls upon the rebels of the day
Whom have many names
Including hero and martyr
Who destruct the peace
With pieces of themselves
Cause tears among the living
With years of repair
To the eyes and memory
The melancholy continues
Must move on without
Human blankets

IV

PREMIUM

Scientist of literature
Ushered into a romantic
Point of view
Stop being an oxymoron
The human meter
Slowly rises
As the bashful seasons progress
Significant direct relationship
Praying that you strive
To be transparent
Grow fond of curiosity
Take pictures with a wide lens
Never been the steady one
But if you like surprises
Then a title shot well earned
Uniform people
Consistently disappointing
It was my usual challenge
To stay away
To not get hurt
When I fall
Save the world
From dry aged me
Unsuccessful martyr
And killer bee
You an option
Without paying a premium

SEA

How much is anonymity worth
Because I have been giving it away
Without charge

After all, it is normal
For an odd person
To make an odd request

The wave ultimately takes
What it wants without consideration
Or pity to how fish feel

Not interested in your salty water
There is nothing left to drink
Then there were none

Save for the quiet
Only the quiet
Across the horizon

To the other side
Where certain events occur
Where intentions are swiftly met
With praise and resolve—
The sun ran away from me
As the sunken settle
To the bottom
Of the
Sea

FLOAT

Hanging heavy
My impressed heart
Desolate open water
Textured with ripples
Mirror above
Threatening grey skies
Like clouds linger
Far horizon on fire
Red-orange burning
Throughout the dark corner
Event storms brew sporadic
And without patience
An ordinary row boat
One to tell the truth
One at peace
Where he belongs
One under circumstance
Under constant duress of the day
Fail once again
Many times over
Ever to stay a float

OIL

Hope sinks to great depths
Joining the bitter company
Of other fallen dreams
On land characters of flesh
As well as the inanimate
Cling to bark and brick
Washing away viable memories
In the aftermath a crude wake
Of debris and black tar
Line forsaken shores
There are disgraced
Walks of life
There are despicable animals
Covered in filth
There are the waned wildlife
And through all this
We must find the tenacity
To survive the term oil

[Dedicated to the 2010 Deepwater Horizon victims and their families]

WATER

Sleep desires
Your dream
Floating in time
Ocean current mattress
Soft rested back
Black sky view
Bruised with blue
Stars ever so dim
Shining through
The still
Breathing under
Water

LIGHT

Vivacity creeps back and forth
Like a pendulum
On a grandfather clock
Still remains our perpetual choice
Gracefully engaged
Art of life assimilates
Into the fair air we breathe
Changing our dull perceptions
Each view a moving mural
Find perspective in landscapes
Find peace in your own brand of park
Find yourself prevail
In a different light

HORIZON

Robust and substantial
The pursuit of anonymity
No one is grabbing the girl
Bound to the railroad track
Just in time
Before the train arrives
These days
No heroes in sight
Absolutely absent
Smokey skies
By and large
The one with the largest database wins
What are you weighting
Invitation to procrastinate
You constantly remind me
Why we are not close friends
Demand more value from your nouns
Especially those that are proper—
People, places and things
Be moved standing still
Beyond event horizon

OTHERSIDE

Gander across the way
Across the yard
Through the pains
Can you keep up
With all of them
Gander into high definition

Our comfort
In the house of cards
Which comes second
To the misuse of applied funds
But what is the real cost
Of throwing stones

Priority responsibility
And the clear choice
Do not always translate
Specifically when you
And meaningful clarity
Are standing on the otherside

WEATHERMAN

To your surprise
And of mine
It could fall
The salt instilled
Into every droplet
Of rain
Which began
In the cumulus clouds
To jump away from the sun
High up
In the corner
Mind of a local weatherman

PARK

Not weathered these eyes
Nostalgic landscape overlay
As young kids play
Skin stained
With bruises
Scrapes and cuts on fresh cut grass
The pass comes all too fast
Subsequently dropped
As the sun glints in the eye
The past so innocent
And forgiving
Could you even
Forgive yourself now
How the time lapse of emotions
Leads one back to the familiar
Serene position
Of an admired
Free spirited park

IRISES

Sitting across from human
Nature takes natural course
Meeting of like minds
This chance heart path
Which curves around
Must not be rushed
Save for this spring
When one finds
To be adrift
In brown irises

POST

Sense of apathy
Coming to an end
On overcast days
No friend of shadow for company
Save for asbestos
Growing on the old fence
Which defines irrelevance
Once again
To the tune
Of comfortable silence
Your eyes speak
Easy over memories
In the present
How you are able
To coax the shy sun
From behind the grey
To shine upon me
Where I await
At post

STEP

Change your scenery or change your eyes
Be realistic
Walk through opportunistic doors
Not into barrier walls
They tend not to open themselves
So you must move
Meet and greet
Get into position!
Perhaps live through it, for now
In time your future shall come
One step will lead to another
One lead to another step

V

SPOKE

We are expected to be
Unscathed no more
By the sharp
Edges of this world
Chipped and worn accordingly
The shift to normality
Let babies cry a tad
Longer to develop
Strong lungs
Debate the great issues of the day
Refute your future presence
Remove the kid gloves
From the secure home
Scars build character
Not security bars
A notion we lack
As a society
Mistakes have their place
Some are your own children
Make the best of them
Know the difference between
Fail safes
And safe fails
We run in circles
Perfectly with a broken spoke

ABOARD

Never claimed to know anything in absolute
Known to me is solely
What I modestly adore and heartily approve of
In my own certain, quirky standards
This subjective concept
Not one person can ever refute
An open mind and kind karma comprise
Of your daily lift ticket
Acknowledge the product of this imaginarium
Whether found to be true
Profound in original thought
Or ferociously false
Is in fact, matters of opinion
Sharing is caring
Welcome value added comments
Information is raw meat prepared as you wish
Be well fed
Passion for the immortal written word
Shared with you
What it does for me
Hope, solace, purpose and meaning are most dear
People follow not because they are lost
Need guidance or seemingly weak
But because it is not always possible
To walk side by side
With others who share

Common beliefs, ideals, and similar goals
Time will tell us where we should be
Time does not know how to lie
For it is the most truthful agent
In any setting or place
We shall take precious time traveling
To new heights and cover great distances
Unbound by boundaries
Limitless in potential
Anything possible with creative minds
In the vast mall of web logs
As the red flag points out
You are here
This train of carts steadily grows
This train of honest passengers grows
This train of thought grows
All aboard

ATONE

Give me a song I can sing to
Risks are vitamins worth taking
After all, three wrongs can make a right
There is always room to break away
Go ahead and dance a turn with me
See how broken bones and hearts
Heal stronger than the sum
Of all previous bonds
From the stone prison
Of remorse
Lungs uncaged now
Hear the sounds so terribly loud
Fear now only being this
Hoarse voice is not
Loud enough to atone

CELADON

Life moves on without me in its wake
The day we caught a rainbow or two
Wind in my dreaded hair
The type of person to always pay a debt to society
So I go for a ride in my mind
While whispering this song

Can't buy time with watches
Can't buy time with watches

We share the same hour
But yours is more valuable
Vicarious living through you my fight now
Don't be afraid to chase
Failure's shadow as I have
Settled, nestled between the walls
Of a castle glazed of celadon

CHARACTER

About time
Ever so
Healing bruised flesh
And all responses
Scars remain to tame
Humility

With humor unifying the foreign
From the soft whisper
Of forgiveness
To the lion roar
Of desire
Noble actions compiled wisely
Speak the name of our given
Immortal character

LOSER

When will November come for me?
The world begins to slow down
Tires and balls of feet seem not to bounce as high
It is at this time
Where fall starts to end
The winter begins to freeze
Memories for keepsake

We have all encountered
Dark hours
The beauty of time is such that
There will be light
In the morning—
Perhaps start walking

Therapists are so reasonable
Where is this voice you speak of
Used to be so human
How I have missed
Bear with me
If I don't try
There is a real chance
That I am going to loser

STRUGGLE

Family ties choking at the neck
Work production straining confined spine
The young tugging at restless legs and tired feet
But what we do must be worth it—
Why else would we do it?
To remember
The reason
Why we put up with physical and mental
People pain
Ease the sufferer
Feel improved
Without exception
There is not one person
In these micro worlds
Without relative struggle

VOICE

Thought of place
And my position
Thought of solitude
And my song
Repeats of offense
Go on about
Aspirations with thrill
Sincerely appreciate hearing
Cause for voice

VAGABOND

Gnash your jagged teeth
Endure the burn
Before violent turn
Of sequence
When the ravenous
Thirst arrives
Feed upon my giving wrist—
Nothing else for me to give
But up
One change reveals
Another revelation
Do onto others as you would
Own self-mutilation
All choices lead to dark alleys
And slippery slopes
Out run the cold sun
On the hunger
That is your being
Dependent upon
Amoral vagabond

DEFERENCE

In walking lines
Dodging puddles
Which bore holes
In stained concrete
Take for granted
What must be earned
Create a divide
Of those who deserve
Severity in lenience
The rest of whom may perish
For lack of deference

RULE

Slaves of cycles
From the biological
To the decision making
Know when to breathe
The heat is becoming
Unbearable
Chest starts to compress
Losing function
Trying hard just to hold
It all together
Corners will not align
Will it ever
The threading is off again
Worst yet
Perhaps even stripped
Going back
Hardware store
Searching for a part
Complete work solution
Obtain unspoken rule

REGIME

Ways of folk
Across the grey pond
Our home country invades
Assembly of repression as a means
To a reciprocal courtesy often denied
Horrific bribes but obliged
Press for change and order over time
These immoral nobles
Social special tea
Which spurs quiet
Among a new dialect regime

VI

REFORM

Genuinely make the most of your presence
Strive to move more water with each stroke
Cover more ground with swift feet
Create space and steal time from the opposed—
We are often our greatest enemy
There are no short cuts
We only cheat ourselves otherwise
Absolutely no substitute for hard work
Savor salty sweat and accomplished ache
Break down and rebuild where necessary
All muscles strengthen when they tear and repair
Bones when they break and reset
The continuum of balance between power
Control is paramount in any situation
Without intelligence and craft
The universal game is already lost—
Court, field, cubical or boardroom
Risk humble beginnings
To gain repetitive and methodical techniques
Of form and reform

REBOUND

Step off the platform
Onto the train
Bags in tow
Reap the benefit

Of the doubt
While thoughts and ideals
Seem to swirl inside
At times leaving

With more questions than
Answers on the mind
Of one traveling from
The state of rebound

SLEEP

Causes a symphony
Of unknown certainty and unrest
Dare press enter
There is no going back now
Said too much
To be honest
Truth of the matter
Should not be ashamed
But I am sick
With what I have done
Stomach
Uneasy
But right
Look upward
Time will tell on your face
And not wrist
Seize this day to make amends
For the past
Perhaps we will never meet again
Would want you with
When I'm gone and that won't happen
Soon enough
Logic
Fool
Let me ask for time
While well into sleep

MODERATION

Importance, like concrete
Should be placed wisely
Throw away
What others cherish
To have and to hold
Tangibles such as colored paper
Or precious metals
Intangibles such as sustained emotions
And fleeting feelings
There are two ends to every spectrum—
Never speak for the totality
Let your recipe for action
Speak for itself
In words
In paint
In wood
In metal
Put it all together
With past experience
And eloquent restraint
Serve with moderation

BLACK AND WHITE

Reflects others
And objects surround
Comprised of all colors
White

The absence of color
Void of existence
Black

Cold is the absence of heat
Frozen in time

Darkness is the absence of light
Empty hole

These concepts are key
To balance out extremes
Without warmth and light of the sun
What do we have—nothing
There is no use or utility
Duty to find the truth
Estimate responsibly
Our existence means
Never quite plain black and white

GREY

On the edge of where dark water greets the lip
Waves keep coming
Good news is that the waves keep coming
Extra weight to the shore
Amounts to dependency
And loosely tied agenda
My sediments exactly
Forgive as the sand
Dig in a gain
Cautious feet
Frequently cold at first—
Take steps and time
Toward the fire
To warm sensitive digits
You never quite trust in yourself fully
You never quite know what will transpire
You never quite walk away with nothing
There is a cost to learning self-value
And parabolic dignity
Over time normality erodes
At abrasive extremities
Serenity sits accompanied by accomplishment
Together gazing at nostalgic
Displays of grey

WEIGHT

Peace inversely related
Available for purchase
Over the counter
At mean street markets
Measured on calibrated digits
Flush the system
Constantly overfill—
Suitcases, homes, selves
Visit a simple time
When plastic in wallets
Are not stones
When the world did not rest
Solely on our tired shoulders
When our mighty limbs
Supported the bearing of life
When we exercised control
When we choose to perceive
Act as though floating
Fog lifts from the air
To reveal certain clarities
Problems dissipate
Bare naked body—
Renewed and revived
Refreshed and alive
By losing an infinitesimal
Amount of weight

CHOICE

Who will be sent down for us
Evil nature
Good spirits
Agitation and misfortune dependent
Upon personal sleep cycles
Search for odd remedies
And natural roots
Often looking toward the East
For uncommon answers
Which doctor or potion will save us
Pipe smoke and needle holes
Tend to dissolve discussion
Suppress solutions
Insolvent behavior
Valuable lessons reside at eye level
Open wide
Process all angles
Of the full picture
Abstain from misreading the harsh
Parallax of the life cylinder
Water levels are taken
At the bottom of the meniscus
And must be recorded
For the responsible
Human experiment

Consider that we are but

The sum of decisions

Durable tools and flesh resources

Used for a fix

The shining key to any daunting mission statement

Not made of any metal alloy

Powerful powder

Brewed liquid

But of strategy and execution in determination

Moral utopian suicide

Attempts result when we choose

Not to listen to our internal or external inputs

Regarding the broad subject

Of the tough and obstructed

Practical choice

GOODS

Prefer the one
Chipped on the shoulder
Blemishes, marks and scars give us character
And memory of
Who we are
Lose importance
Gain that which is more valuable
Temporary epiphanies are lasting
Lose an arm
Gain perseverance and patience
Lose hope but gain faith
Lose sight but gain vision
Lose hearing but gain understanding
Lose someone, gain yourself
The blind may not choose to see
The deaf may not choose to hear
We assume need in order to exist
Society holds dull notions
We are all eclectic types and sizes
Highly unique and consciously brittle
That is a threat
Choose to act foolishly
Do without having
Your way
Our homes but made
Of sugar cubes and candy glass

Break away from the mold
Without breaking down
Stand for just cause
Absolute passion
Individual art
Persistent mystery
Selfless legacy
Finding oneself is never
A finished journey
But place secure
On the tolerant universal shelf
Of damaged goods

APOCALYPSE

Destiny theory

Forgone

Inhabitant morale

Questioning

Equilibrium restoration

Domino

Human condition

Return

Nano measurement

Surprise

Optimistic investment

Venture

Handmade fortune

Vitality

Crystal ball

Apocalypse

VII

ENTER VIEW

Online service query match
Career building monster workout
Impressive honest linen paper
Meaningful experience journal list

Monetary cranium hunter versus
Protocol obedient corporate recruiter
Anxious judgement appointment schedule
Ungraded two way street

Audio visual interrogation techniques
Dangerous risk giving game
Memory induced mistake agitator

Strategic verbal defense guard
Rhetoric truth be told
Fortune teller credit manager
Point of no return

Invalidated haughty executive decision
Confidence determination news letter
Molecule dissection break down
Self assessment enter view

SOLIDARITY

A fraudulent scheme
Harboring felon
Under cover
Gracious benefactor

Mask intentions
Personas fascinating
Disguise true essence
Surface perceived impression

Initial review
Suggests familiarity
Further reconnaissance
Reveals otherwise surprise

Pieced plywood utilize
Warm woods as veneer
Bland concrete uses
Elegant porous stones

Employ insincere swagger
Sweet nothings
Deficient acting
Create calculations

Scenes cast
Drill deep
Image is nothing
Without substance

Facades cover truth
Immense power
Portray honor
Epitomize solidarity

BITTER WINTER

Comes now bitter winter
Unsympathetic oblique splinter
Prophetic hands of time
Insubordinate coup alliance

Search party rescue pantomime
Black snow driven defiance
Rising soul expired
White sheet bed cover
Utility shovel meat lover

Dried leaves on fire
Presents breed villainous reason
Redundant broken whistle
Pine scent in season

WAKE

Still as upright daffodils
Feeding upon opaque matter

Portray with ominous light
Overcast cloud cover hovering
Ruins thine eye site

Coordinate grey stones land
Significant right angle demand
Conscientious peace dies down
Except when strangers present

Annual rate of return
Decomposing cupcake favor
Savor stick wax collection
Parallel flesh fathom difference
Body lying a wake

PROLOGUE

Rescue me
From somber subjects
Sour outlook
Ever improving
No one speaks
Like you under water
Swimming now in close circles
To avoid the cold shivers
In awe of the raw
Energy it requires
To float back
To where we once were
On the stained wood
Dock of certainty
Promise and prologue

SWANS

Elephant reflections
In the blue water
Dead trees getting taller
The live desert
With steep red cliffs
Hanging on the outskirts of
Human nature's wardrobe
These dimensional clouds
What do I see in them?
In any place?
Perverse man
At any rate
Once my heart
Is found
Boat shall move
From this sentiment sand
And stay in motion
Be quiet!
Nothing will stop us
Arriving at mute swans

GANDER

At times, the issue at hand rises
In front of your red face
And constantly on the mind
But it does not manifest
Or become present
Try not to remember
Only then will it become true
Instead look forward to a better time
In the future
Can't tread to the past
Keep fast forwarding
Might take a while to get out of this slump
Write about the moon, the stars—
That which cannot harm you
Fascinations and magic
That do not desert
With a quick look outside
Ever ready for your gander

HUG

People evolve. A necessary and certain change. This constant tide makes you worried of new relationships and weary about the ones which you are currently involved. Who will be standing near you in the future? More importantly—exactly where will they stand.

For this very reason, savor every minute with the people you hold dear now! Should those times end, abruptly or slowly, and for absolutely any reason, know that they did matter. Know they left a mark on your soul and a sizable difference in your life. Continue. Continue.

Mystery is neither an ally nor enemy, rather, what you make of it. The winter makes you more cautious. Yet, the onslaught of inevitable holidays brings out partial vulnerability in a person. Solitude should not always be so selfish. Hug yourself first, then hug others, and often hug.

PATH

Through the ominous
Arm in arm as if with three
Spirits high and free
From the chagrin of daily tribunals
A pair braving the present pour
Which reflects off shields
Of faith and comfort
And onward to the yellow
Halo glow of street lamps
Then beyond
Tonight we walk
On this miracle night path

ASHORE

With Love frequent as the relentless tide
Laughter gentle as the cool wind
Hand in hand
Against the meaningful grains of sand
The important shells
We often search for
Tend to be the familiar faces
Of family and friends ashore

FAVOR

You were carried on my sure shoulder
Rocking infinite nights
Like a boulder weeping
Begged my legs to keep us safe
To brace up high
Arms locked and loaded
Wearing fatigues

Strength found
Deep down in the core
Bound by blood
Official chore
And moral code
Old nursery rhymes
Fairy tales recited

And often repeated
Memories of perseverance
And touching kinship
To be one's savior
To have a wise man
One elated day
Return the favor

WORLD

The arrival of prevalent blessings
Shrouded in blankets of affection
Reflected off the glistening faces of
Our anticipated family and loved ones
You bring a tenderness to a harsh world
And subdue the resounding
Cries of adversity
A sight to discern—
Radiant skin, adorable face and body
Make me smile while tears
Brim at my eyes
Where I will never
Forget this magical moment
Ever on my reign
Until I see you again
In our next world

[Dedicated to James Reed Ly and his families]

LEGACY

An admirable year in the rear-view
A time to review
The blessings
Of precious characters
Around the crackling
Of busy fire
A new beginning
For us to make a difference
In our fortunate legacy

CLOUDS

Cracks remind one that
They are damaged
But not broken
How wings might fly
Although not straight
Even with the wind at our backs
And so we tend
To lay low to the ground
For you don't see
Too many of us
High in the clouds

SURROUND

A night light need not shine
For the Love of my beloved parents is shown
A blanket need not cover bare skin
For my home is full of warmth
And I will never be lonely
For support and wisdom ever
Surround

INDEX OF TITLES

www.ingramcontent.com/pod-product-compliance
Lightning Source LLC
Chambersburg PA
CBHW032005040426
42448CB00006B/487